INDIA

140 MILLION YEARS OF HISTORY

S. MAHESH

TAKSHAŚILA MUDRANA

ISBN: 978-81-970534-0-5
First published 2025

Published by

TAKSHAŚILA MUDRANA

Imprint of Parjanya Consultants Private Limited
Hyderabad, INDIA

www.takshasilamudrana.com
contact@takshasilamudrana.com
Printed in India

To all my teachers

India: 140 Million Years of History

Preface

For someone unfamiliar with geography, a world map might appear as nothing more than a mosaic of colours. Yet, each colour represents more than just a geographical boundary – it embodies an identity. An identity that shapes people's lives, influences their allegiances and conflicts.

Nations have been built and defended in the name of these identities, and history has witnessed moments when humanity itself was sacrificed at their altar. However, the very idea of dividing land into distinct national territories is a relatively recent development – a construct of the human mind aimed at creating exclusive zones.

Before the dawn of human history, none of the world's existing countries – except one – had an independent marker. The lone exception was India. The landmass now called India (the subcontinent or tectonic plate) has had a uniquely continuous identity for an astonishing 140 million years.

India's journey began millions of years ago when it got separated from Gondwanaland and set forth on a collision course with Eurasia, giving birth to the Himalayas. This event shaped not just changed the subcontinent's topography but also its climate.
The rise of the Indus Valley Civilisation marked the beginning of India's structured societies. The emergence of the Mahajanapadas, the

conquests of Magadha, the unification under the Mauryan Empire, and the cultural zenith of the Guptas defined the classical era. While the southern dynasties such as the Cholas, Cheras, and Pandyas, played a crucial role in maritime trade and cultural diffusion. Buddhism and Jainism offered alternative spiritual pathways, while interactions with Greek, Persian, and Central Asian invaders added new dimensions to Indian polity, art, and culture.

The medieval period witnessed both grandeur and turbulence, with the rise and fall of the Rajputs, the Delhi Sultanate, and the Vijayanagara Empire. The arrival of Islam reshaped India's socio-political landscape, leading to centuries of interaction, conflict, and synthesis. The Mughals left a mark on governance, architecture, and artistic traditions. However, the empire's decline paved the way for the emergence of new powers such as the Marathas and the Sikhs.

The colonial era heralded another transformative phase. Trading companies became the rulers of the country. The resistance against foreign rule took many forms, which culminated in the end of British rule in 1947.

This book serves as a tribute to the resilience of a civilisation that has continuously adapted, reinvented, and flourished. It provides an essential foundation for anyone seeking to understand India's vast history, offering a glimpse into the dynamism that has shaped its journey through time.

Umamaheshwar Singoji
writing as S. Mahesh

Each region in India has different pronunciation for names or words used in ancient India. Therefore, the words used in this book have spellings that reflect their pronunciation in Sanskrit.

India: 140 Million Years of History

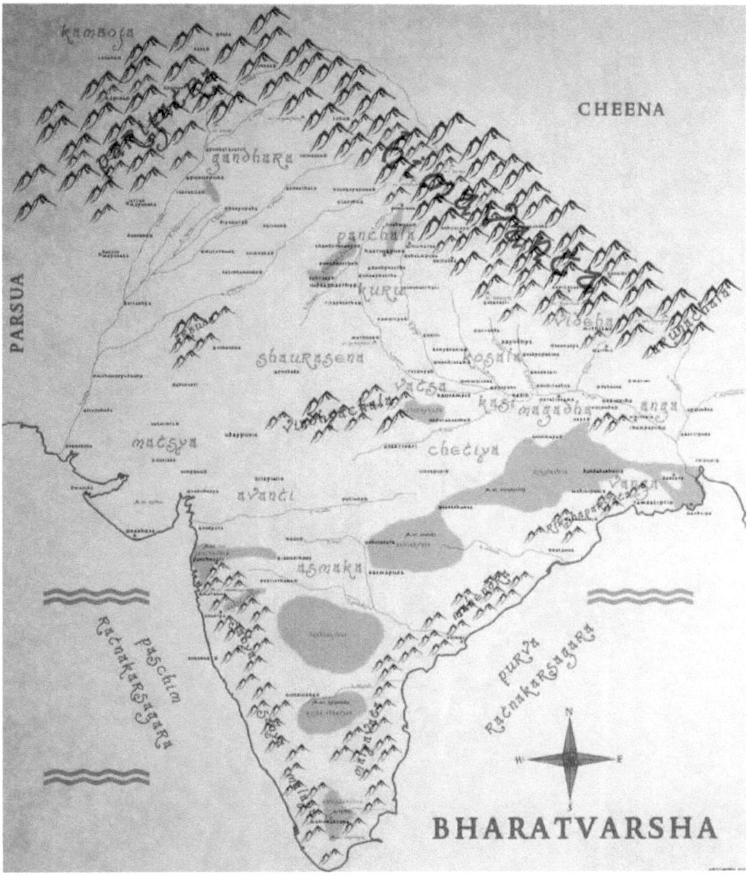

Uttaram Yat Samudrasya Himaadreshchaiva Dakshinam
Varsham Tad Bhaaratam Naama Bhaaratee Yatra Santatih

The country that lies to the north of the ocean and to the south of snowy mountains is called Bharata as there dwell the descendants of Bharat

India: 140 Million Years of History

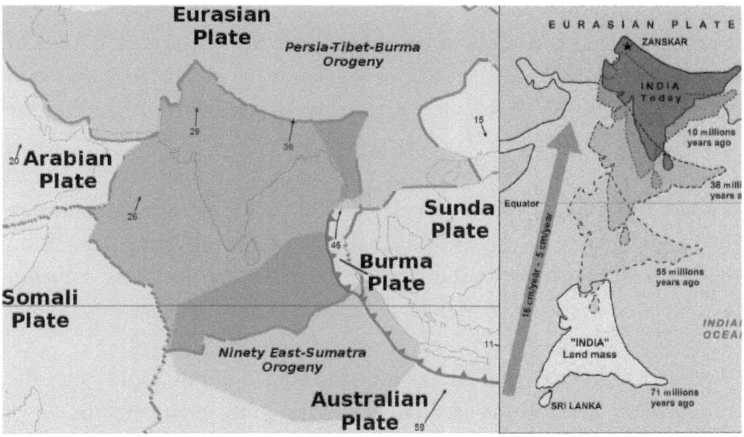

Split, Lava, and Collision

More than 140 million (14 crore) years ago, India was part of an immensely large supercontinent called Gondwanaland, which consisted of today's Global South, including Africa, South America, Antarctica, and Australia. However, it slowly began to drift away from the mainland.

Twenty million (two crore) years after the drift began, India broke off from the supercontinent and started its northward journey towards Eurasia. Along its route, it left Madagascar and the Seychelles behind. The movement of this massive landmass over the Réunion hotspot triggered volcanic activity, which initiated the formation of what we now know as the Deccan Plateau.

About 65 million (6.5 crore) years ago, an asteroid entered the Earth's atmosphere and struck Mexico. Its impact was felt in India, triggering massive volcanic eruptions in the Deccan. The dust spewed by the asteroid's impact, combined with the release of enormous amounts of sulphur dioxide from the Deccan volcanoes, plunged the Earth into an ice age, leading to the mass extinction of life forms, including the dinosaurs.

Fifteen million (1.5 crore) years later, India collided with the Eurasian Plate, giving rise to the great Himalayas, extending from the Hindu Kush in Afghanistan to the Arakan Yoma in Burma. This collision also created the world's highest tableland, Tibet.

As the Earth recovered from the twin-impact catastrophe and life rebounded, civilisations gradually emerged in different regions.

Birth of civilisation

In India, a unique civilisation began developing in the Indus River Valley around 7,000 years ago. It was a sophisticated society with well-planned cities, bustling trade, and commerce. However, it declined around 5,000 years ago as summer rains became unpredictable.

Following the decline of the Indus civilisation, people transitioned to a village-based lifestyle, a period popularly known among historians as the Vedic Age. Over time, Indian civilisation shifted from the Indus-Saraswati region to the Gangetic Plains. The use of iron increased agricultural productivity, while expanding trade and commerce led to the emergence of new cities. This period became known

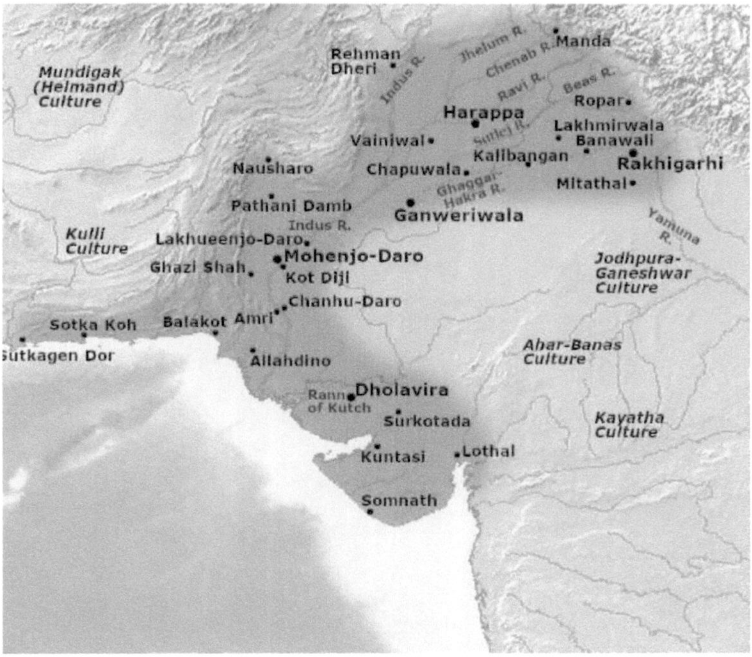

as the era of the 16 Mahajanapadas, a collection of 16 powerful kingdoms centred around major cities.

Pre-Mauryan period

During the Mahajanapada era, North and South India were separated by the vast Dandakaranya forest in the rugged Deccan region, stretching between the Godavari and Krishna rivers. While the Mahajanapadas flourished in the North, the South was home to the Cholas, Cheras, and Pandyas, who maintained thriving external trade networks with Europe.

The era of large empires began around 500 BCE when Magadha con-

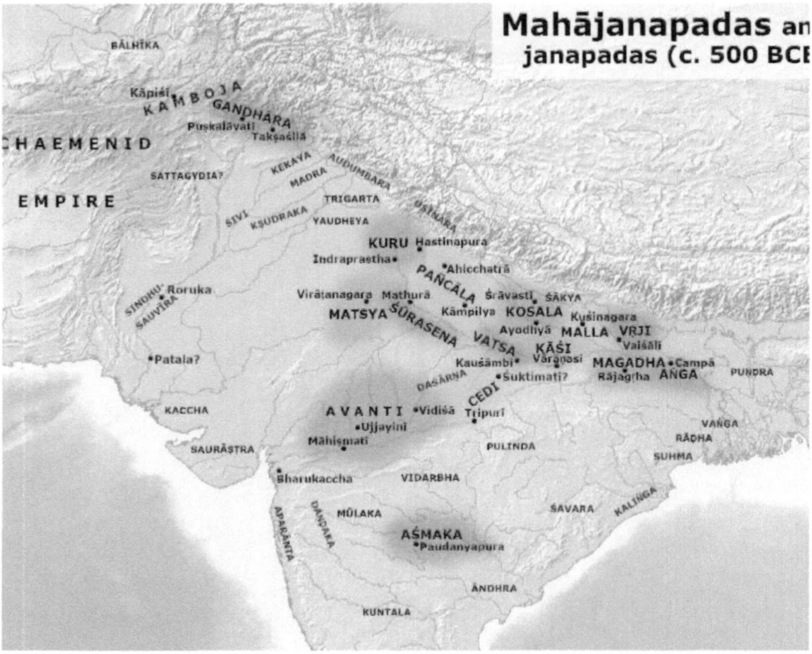

quered Anga and incorporated it into its territory. Over time, Magadha expanded its dominion, absorbing several of the older Mahajanapadas. On the religious front, two new religions – Buddhism and Jainism – emerged, offering peaceful alternatives to the Vedic religion.

Mauryan period

When Alexander of Macedonia arrived in India, Magadha was a vast empire that struck fear into the hearts of Greek soldiers. However, Chanakya, a teacher at Takshashila University, was not pleased. He aspired to build an even stronger empire that could protect India from foreign invasions. Through a web of alliances and strategic

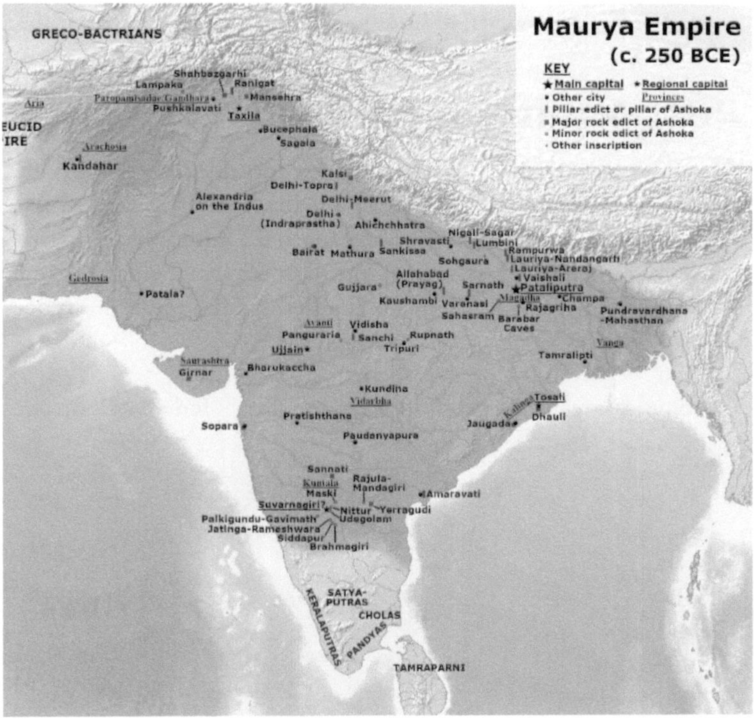

manoeuvres, he helped his student Chandragupta in establishing the Mauryan Empire. by defeating the Magadha emperor Mahapadma Nanda, who was the most powerful ruler in India. Chandragupta expanded his empire from Bactria (Uzbekistan) and Gandhara (Kandahar) in the northwest to the Cauvery River in the south.

The Mauryan Empire reached its peak under Ashoka's rule when defeated Kalinga, but his pacifist policies sowed the seeds of its decline. However, he contributed the most spreading Indian culture beyond the traditional boundaries of India by propagating Buddhism. After Ashoka's death, the empire fragmented into several smaller states. The south, however, did not come under the direct rule of the Maurya rule.

Post-Mauryan period

While the traditional Chola-Chera-Pandya trio ruled the land south of the Cauvery, the Andhra-based Satavahana dynasty dominated the southern peninsula between the Narmada and Cauvery rivers.
Pushyamitra Shunga assassinated the last Mauryan emperor and established the Shunga Empire in northern India, while the Indo-Greeks held sway over the Takshashila region.

The Shungas made every effort to prevent the Indo-Greeks from

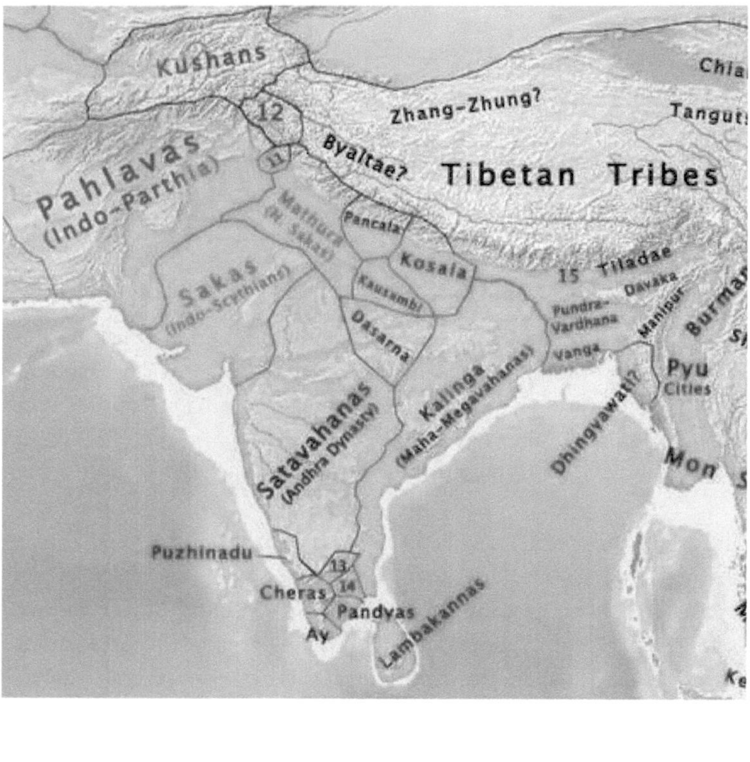

advancing into the Gangetic plains, but they could not hold them back for long. The Indo-Scythians, or Sakas, made deep inroads into India, reaching present-day Rajasthan, Gujarat, and Uttar Pradesh as far as Mathura.

The Satavahanas, however, successfully defended the southern peninsula, which included present-day Maharashtra, Telangana, Andhra Pradesh, and Karnataka, from foreign invasions during the 500 years of turbulence that followed the fall of the Mauryan Empire.

The traditional southern trio continued its dominance south of the Cauvery, remaining largely unaffected by northern conflicts.

Gupta period

After more than a century of political fragmentation, during which the Kushanas and Indianised Western Satraps dominated the north-western region, the Gupta Empire was established. Considered the golden age of Indian history, the empire unified the northern and western regions, ushering in an era of peace and prosperity.

However, the southern Deccan peninsula became fragmented. The Vakatakas ruled the Deccan Plateau up to the Tungabhadra River, the Abhiras controlled the Malwa region, and the Kadambas held sway over present-day Karnataka. South of the Cauvery River, the rule of the traditional trio ended, giving rise to a new dynasty – the Kalabhras. From Kanchi, the Kalabhras ruled Tamil Nadu and Kerala for 300 years.

The Kidarites, or Hunas from Samarkand, who claimed to be the successors of the Kushan Empire, attempted to invade India. They became a persistent threat to the Gupta Empire, disrupting its trade and commerce with the Roman Empire.

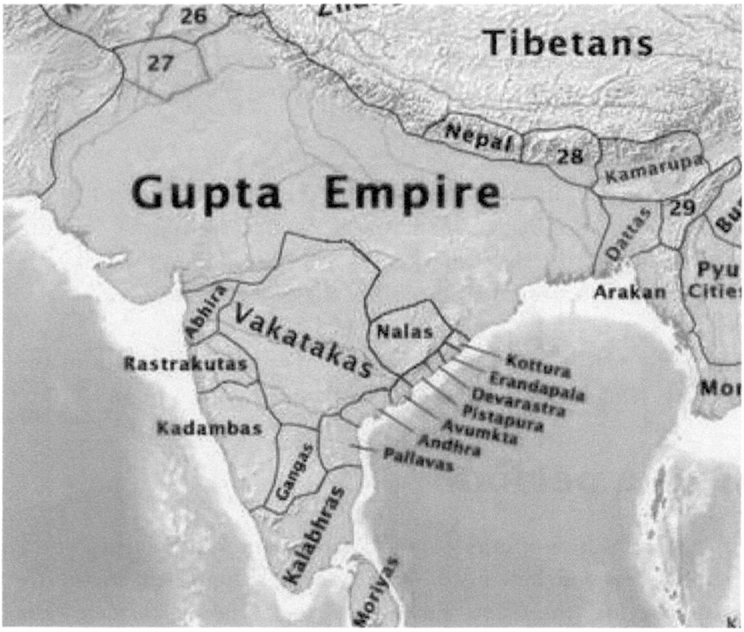

After several decades of pressure from the Hunas, internal attacks by the Pushyamitras from south of the Narmada, and succession disputes, the Gupta Empire weakened and eventually fragmented into smaller kingdoms. In post-Gupta India, the only significant power was the Chalukyas in the Deccan. South of the Cauvery River, Kalabhra rule ended, and the Pallavas rose to prominence. Older dynasties such as the Cholas, Cheras, and Pandyas re-emerged.

Post-Gupta period

Another branch of the Huns, called the Alchon Huns, who replaced the Kidarites in Central Asia, demolished 1,000 Buddhist monasteries in Takshashila, an impact from which the ancient centre of learn-

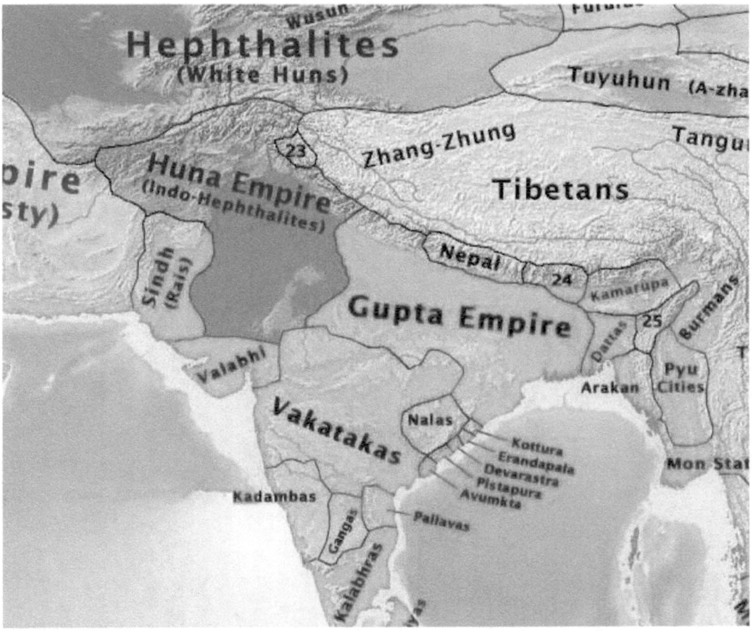

ing never recovered. The Alchon Huns overran Indian territory as far as present-day Uttar Pradesh and Madhya Pradesh. However, they were defeated by an alliance of smaller kingdoms led by the Malwa king Yashodharman.

After his victory, Yashodharman reigned supreme in the north during his lifetime. The south remained relatively calm, with stable empires such as the Chalukyas, Pallavas, Cheras, and Pandyas.

Harsha period

In the seventh century, Harshavardhana of the Pushyabhuti dynasty in Haryana built an extensive empire in the north, spanning present-day Delhi, Uttar Pradesh, Uttarakhand, Bihar, Jharkhand, and Bengal.

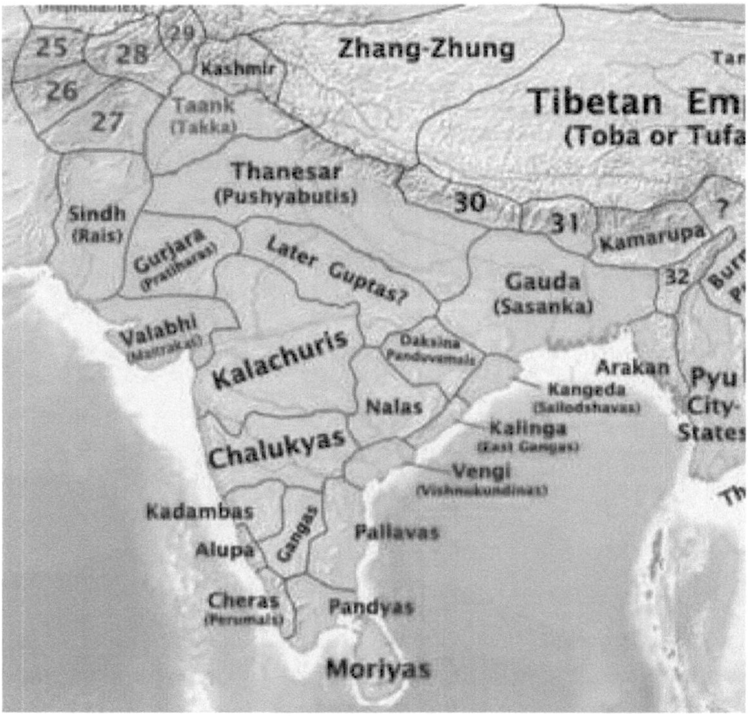

This was the last Hindu empire in north India before the advent of Muslim rulers. In the peninsula, the Chalukyas and Pallavas were engaged in a struggle for supremacy.

During Harshavardhana's rule, a new empire arose in the west of India, whose followers were driven by religious zeal to expand their influence. Within a few years, the Arabs overran Persia and parts of Africa, forming the Islamic Caliphate. For the next 100 years, the Arabs were preoccupied with internal dissensions. The first Arab incursion into India was recorded in Sindh in 649, but it was unsuccessful.

After Harshavardhana's death, the north once again fragmented. However, after a few years, Yashovarman of Kannauj rose to prominence. As Persia fell and internal conflicts within the Caliphate subsided, the Arabs launched another invasion, successfully occupying Sindh in 711.

Triple power

Following the deaths of Yashovarman and the Kashmiri king Lalitaditya, the Gurjara-Pratiharas gained ascendancy in north India, while the Rashtrakutas replaced the Chalukyas as the dominant power in central and western India. In the south, the Cholas re-entered the power struggle, while the Pallavas and Cheras maintained their influence. In the east, the Pala dynasty consolidated its control.

In the northwest, Muslim kingdoms emerged in Sindh and Multan, while the Turk Shahis in Kabul remained the last vestige of Indian civilisation in the border regions.

Between 724 and 810, the Arabs made several attempts to invade India, but multiple kingdoms successfully blocked them. In the north, Nagabhata of the Pratihara dynasty defeated a major Arab expedition in Malwa. From the south, Vikramaditya II sent Avanijanashraya Pulakeshin, to defeat the Arabs in Gujarat. Later, in 776 CE, a naval expedition by the Arabs was defeated by the Saindhava naval fleet under Agguka I.

These defeats halted Arab expansion into India, ultimately leading to the overthrow of Arab rulers in Sindh and the rise of local Muslim dynasties, the Soomras and Sammas. The Buddhist Turk Shahis, who came to power in Kabul and Gandhara, successfully resisted Muslim invasions from Central Asia for 250 years. When they could no longer

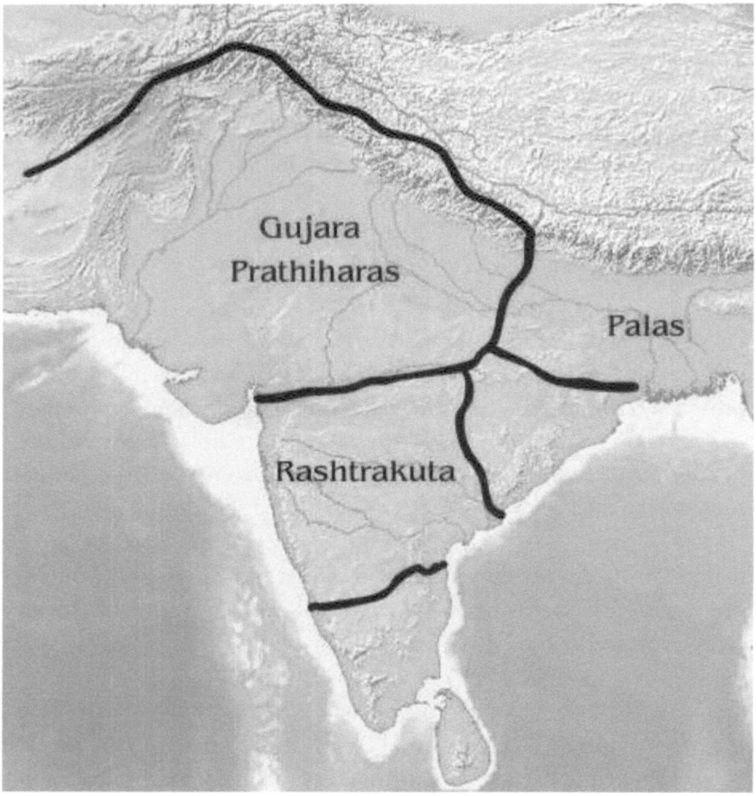

hold out, the Hindu Shahis, supported by the Gurjara-Pratiharas, took up the fight against Muslim incursions from Samarkand.

For the next 100 years, India was dominated by three major empires: the Gurjara-Pratiharas in the north, the Rashtrakutas in the south, and the Palas in the east. While these three empires engaged in pre-emptive strikes against one another to maintain a balance of power, Muslim forces in Central Asia were consolidating and threatening the last remaining Hindu outpost – the Hindu Shahi kingdom in Kabul and Kandahar.

The Gurjara-Pratiharas experienced a golden age under Mihira Bhoja. His empire prospered, the Arabs were kept at bay by the Hindu Shahis, and the Rashtrakutas suffered territorial losses under their less aggressive ruler, Amoghavarsha. However, Bhoja's death triggered internal conflicts over succession. The Rashtrakutas, wary of the new Gurjara-Pratihara monarch Mahipala stabilising his rule, launched a preemptive attack in 916, sacking Kanyakubja (Kannauj) and severely damaging the power and prestige of the imperial Pratiharas.

Over the next two decades, the bond between the Gurjara-Pratiharas and their feudatories weakened. In 940, the Rashtrakutas once again defeated Kannauj. This attack proved fatal, effectively destroying the power of Kannauj. Its feudatories in Rajasthan, Gujarat, Malwa, and Punjab became de facto independent, maintaining only nominal allegiance to the imperial Pratiharas.

In the south, the Rashtrakutas were eventually replaced by their feudatories, the Chalukyas of Kalyani. The Cholas consolidated their power by defeating the Pandyas. While a new ruler, Jata Choda Bhima, emerged to dominate much of the east coast, he was ultimately defeated due to internal dissensions, backed by the Cholas.

The downfall of the Gurjara-Pratiharas in the north and the Rashtrakutas in the south marked the end of the ancient epoch in Indian history and ushered in the mediaeval period, characterised by fragmented political power and increasing Islamic incursions into the Indian heartland.

Weakened frontier

The rise of a new power in Ghazni under its slave ruler, Sabuktigin, and the declining strength of the Gurjara-Pratiharas altered the dynamics of India's western frontier. The Hindu Shahis, now without support from the Indian heartland, were left to defend themselves alone.

Between 988 and 1001, three battles took place between the Hindu Shahis and the Ghaznavid rulers – two under Sabuktigin and the final one under his son, Mahmud. The Hindu Shahis were defeated

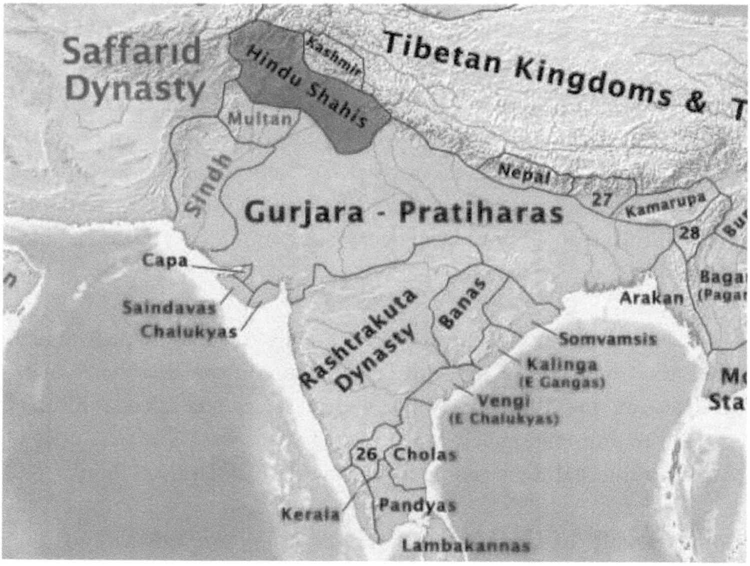

in all three, allowing the Ghaznavids to occupy Indian territory up to the western banks of the Indus River. By 1008, Mahmud had defeated the last Hindu Shahi ruler in Lahore and extended his domain to the Sutlej River.

Meanwhile, in the Indian heartland, the Gurjara-Pratiharas had lost control over their feudatories, leading to the fragmentation of the northern empire into several independent kingdoms in Rajasthan, Awadh, Bundelkhand, Gujarat, and Malwa.

Fragmented north

The new major kingdoms that emerged included the Chahamanas of Shakambhari (Chauhans of Ajmer), the Chaulukyas of Gujarat, the Chandelas of Jejakabhukti (Bundelkhand), the Paramaras of Mandapa Durga (Mandu), and the Gahadavalas of Kanyakubja (Kannauj). However, none of these kingdoms matched the former glory or power of the Gurjara-Pratiharas in the north or the Rashtrakutas in the south.

The south, however, was peaceful and remained prosperous. The Chalukyas of Kalyani ruled most of the land that lay south of the

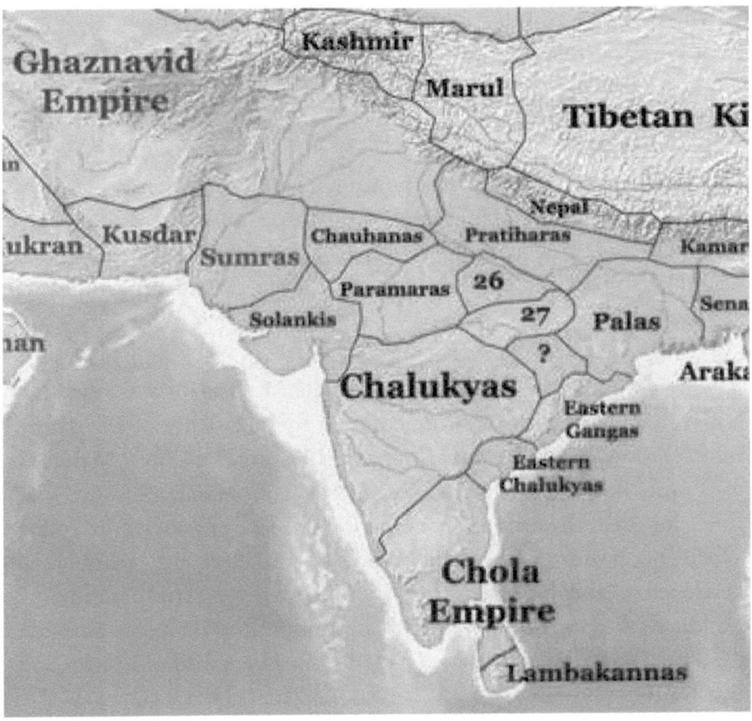

Vindhyas, emerging as the largest empire in India. The Cholas grew in power by installing a puppet regime in Andhra and maintaining a friendly regime in Kalinga. Chola king Rajaraja pushed back his border with the Chalukyas to the Tungabhadra. He strengthened Chola naval power to acquire northern Lanka, the Lakshadweep, and the Maldives islands. The east was also stable, with the Pala Empire standing strong in Bengal.

Muslim raids

In 1015, Mahmud of Ghazni sought to extend his rule further into India. His first target was Kashmir, but inclement weather forced him to abandon the siege and proceed towards Kannauj, which had been the imperial capital of northern India. When he arrived at Kannauj, it was a pale shadow of its ancient glory. Its ruler submitted without a fight.

Having heard of the riches in Mathura, he led his army into the holy town of Lord Krishna. He destroyed thousands of temples and smelted golden idols. The main golden idol yielded 8,300 miskals, or 35 kg, of gold. He returned to Ghazni with a booty carried on a hundred camels.

After a few years, the Chandella ruler attacked Kannauj and killed the last Gurjara-Pratihara ruler for accepting the suzerainty of an Islamic ruler, erasing the last vestiges of imperial history. This drew Mahmud back into India, where he subdued several kingdoms. For the first time, he used firearms such as naphtha-laden projectiles in India. When he heard of the importance of the Somnath temple, he destroyed it and looted its wealth. While on his return journey, a Hindu took revenge on Mahmud by misguiding his army through the Thar Desert, where the majority of his soldiers died of hunger and thirst.

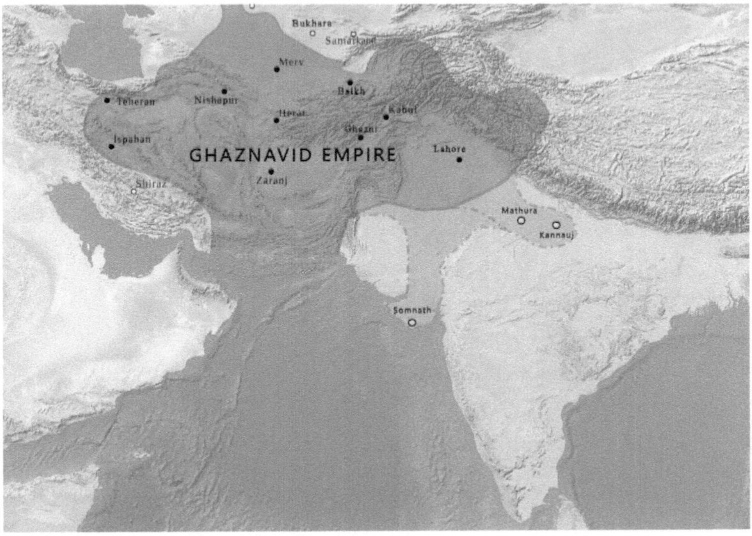

Unlike other Islamic conquests that would later come into India, Mahmud of Ghazni did not install any Muslim governors in the defeated territories but allowed their incumbent rulers to function under his suzerainty. This preserved the Hindu character of the Indian polity for another 150 years.

Chola Lake

In the south, Rajaraja Chola's son, Rajendra, took Chola power to its height. He became the only Indian monarch to expand his territory overseas through naval expeditions to parts of Burma and the Malay Peninsula, now part of Malaysia and Indonesia. He launched a military expedition along the east coast and defeated the kings of Odisha and Bengal, bringing the entire Bay of Bengal coastline under his domination and thus renaming the eastern sea the Chola Lake.

Three years after he plundered Somnath, Mahmud of Ghazni died of

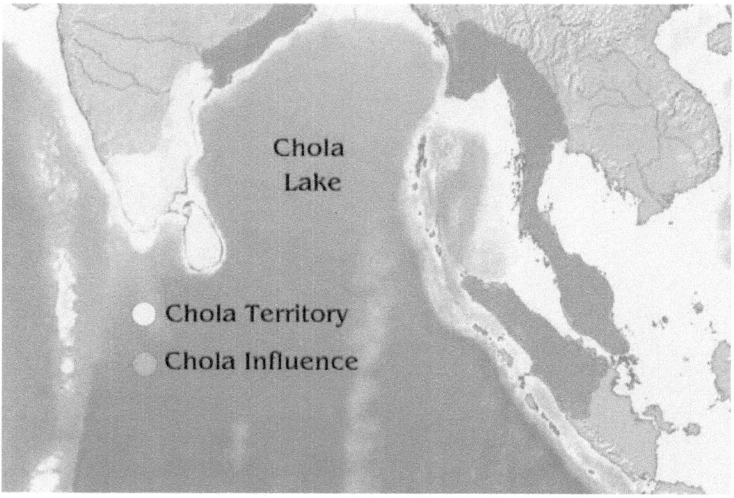

malaria in 1030. Over the next ten years, his sons fought among themselves and lost most of their territories in Persia and Central Asia to the Oghuz Turks' Seljuk Empire. The Seljuks, content with ruling areas west of the Hindu Kush, left the territory from Lahore to Ghazni untouched. However, within the next ten years, the Ghazni Empire collapsed. Since the Seljuks were not interested in India and the Ghoris had not yet risen to power, India was spared from a Muslim threat for the next 125 years.

Divided north

As the north was divided among multiple kingdoms, they resumed their old game of jostling for supremacy. Among the four major kingdoms, the Chandelas were the first to fall out of the race. The Paramaras of the Malwa region and the Chahamanas of Rajasthan emerged as formidable military powers. The Gahadavalas of Kannauj, the Kalachuris of Chedi, and the Chaulukyas of Gujarat were also significant powers with immense prosperity.

In the south, the Chalukyas of Kalyani and the Cholas were the pre-eminent powers, with the Krishna River as their frontier. However, the Chalukyas of Kalyani and the Paramaras of Malwa were locked in a contest for supremacy over the land between the Godavari and Narmada rivers, replacing the earlier feud between the Rashtrakutas and the Gurjara-Pratiharas. The Paramara kingdom, already weakened by invasions from the southern Chalukyas, suffered a severe blow when the rulers of Gujarat and Chedi launched a joint attack. This twin assault led to the kingdom's virtual downfall, leaving central India without a major power and allowing the Chahamanas of Rajasthan to emerge as the de facto dominant force in the north.

The south, however, remained stable. With the southern frontier at peace, Chalukya Vikramaditya launched a northern expedition to reclaim supremacy, following in the footsteps of the Rashtrakutas. The weakened northern kingdoms were unable to stop his advance, and he reached Kannauj unopposed. After symbolically occupying the city, he proceeded to attack the Pala Empire in eastern India, the last surviving remnant of ancient Indian imperial power.

Vikramaditya defeated the Pala Empire, which had already been weakened by attacks from the Kalachuris of Chedi. This defeat pushed the Pala frontier further east, paving the way for the rise of the Sena dynasty, originally from Karnataka, which established its rule in the Radha region, corresponding to present-day Kolkata.

Following this northern campaign, the Chalukyas of Kalyani emerged as the supreme power in India. However, internal strife between Vikramaditya and his jealous elder brother, Someshvara, put a halt to the Chalukyan military expansion. Although Vikramaditya eventually overcame the power struggle, it strengthened his feudatories, including the southern Kalachuris, the Kakatiyas of Warangal, and the

Hoysalas of Dwarasamudra (modern Mysore). While these vassals remained loyal to Vikramaditya, his successors failed to uphold his legacy. The Kakatiyas revolted, establishing an independent kingdom in Warangal, the Hoysalas declared independence, and the Kalachuris occupied Kalyani, bringing an end to the Western Chalukya dynasty.

The Cholas, on the other hand, suffered a decline after the death of Rajendra Chola's son, Rajadhiraja, in 1052. Although they lost Vengi, their northern dependency in Andhra, they regained influence by supporting Chalukya Vikramaditya during his conflict with Someshvara. However, with no direct successors from Rajaraja the Great, the Chola throne passed to Kulothunga, the son of a Chola princess and an Eastern Chalukyan prince. Lacking the aggressive leadership of Rajaraja's lineage, the Chola Empire failed to assert its dominance despite being the largest power in India at the time.

Muslim north, Hindu south

By 1175, Mohammad of Ghori and his brother had firmly established themselves on India's western frontier and set out on an eastern campaign. His first target was Gujarat, but after crossing the desert, his army was thoroughly exhausted and suffered a defeat.

Eleven years later, Ghori attacked India again, this time through the Khyber Pass. A confederate army of Rajput kingdoms, led by Prithviraj Chauhan, faced Ghori and defeated him. However, after the win, Prithviraj's relations with other kingdoms deteriorated, and he neglected military preparedness after the dismissal of his minister.

When Ghori returned to the banks of the Indus a year later, northern India failed to unite against him. Although Prithviraj confronted the invader, Ghori resorted to deceit, launching a surprise attack at night and routing the defending forces.

Unlike Mahmud of Ghazni, Ghori appointed his representatives as the sultans of Delhi for his newly acquired territories in India, heralding a new era of Muslim rule in Indian history. Later, he dismembered several Hindu kingdoms, expanding the Delhi Sultanate into the preeminent power in the north. After Ghori was assassinated in 1206, the Delhi Sultanate severed its ties with the Ghoris.

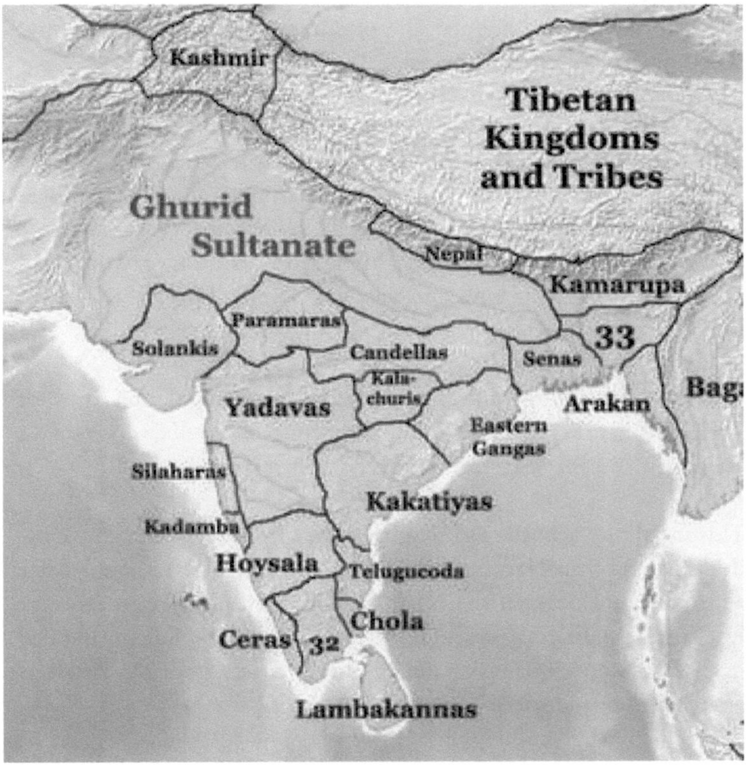

The Delhi Sultanate's first sultan, Qutbuddin Aibak, could be considered the true founder of Muslim power in India. He neutralised the

Rajput threat in the north. Native kingdoms in Rajasthan, Awadh, Bundelkhand, Malwa, and Gujarat were no longer in a position to raise the banner of revolt for some time.

During his rule, the Muslims secured their greatest prize: Bihar and Bengal. These regions, with their vast tracts of fertile land irrigated by the Ganga River, were peaceful and offered a steady source of revenue to Delhi, helping to counter the persistent threat from the Rajput kingdoms in the north and west.

Despite the prowess displayed by the Pala Empire in ancient India, Bihar and Bengal were completely unprepared to handle the Muslim invasion. A zamindar of two villages, Ikhtiyaruddin Muhammad Bakhtiyar, overran Bihar and burned down centuries-old universities and Buddhist monasteries. Later, his 18-horse raiding party stormed the palace of the Sena king unchallenged, forcing the king to flee for safety.

Internal intrigues and the threat posed by the marauding army of Genghis Khan kept the Delhi Sultanate unstable. Delhi witnessed 11 sultans in 100 years, averaging less than 10 years per ruler.

This instability kept the Delhi Sultans away from the south. The kingdoms south of the Narmada River remained safe. The Yadava dynasty ruled the land between the Narmada and Krishna rivers – more or less corresponding to present-day Maharashtra. The Kakatiyas ruled over what is now Telangana and Andhra Pradesh, while the Hoysalas governed the land south of the Krishna River.

The downfall of the Chola Empire began after its shocking defeat at the hands of the Pandyas in 1215. The loss triggered several revolts, which gradually led to the end of Chola rule by 1279. The Pandyas replaced the Cholas in the Tamil region, marking the end of the last remnant of India's classical age and the ends ancient history in all regions of the country.

Muslim empire

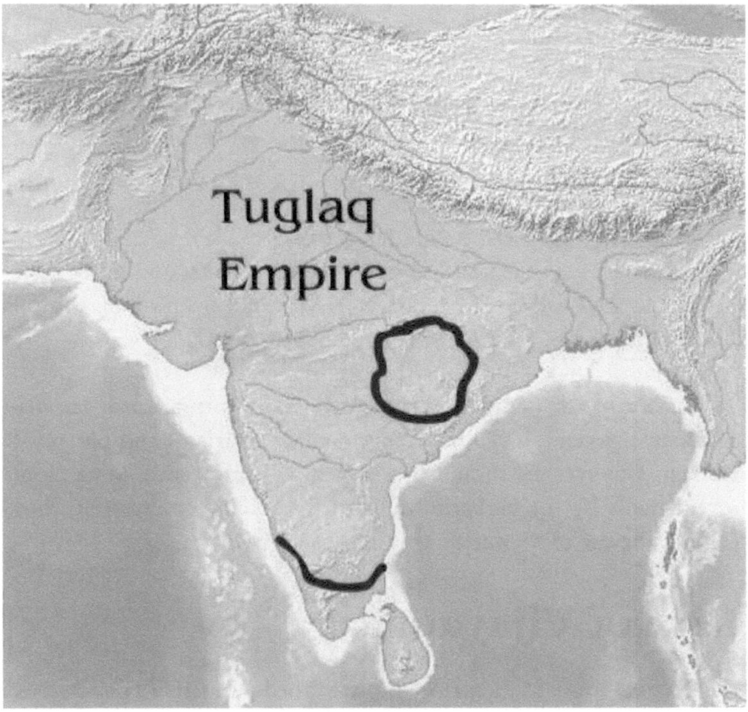

The rise of Alauddin Khalji, the highly ambitious nephew of Sultan Jalal-ud-din Khalji, was the defining event of the 13th and 14th centuries in India. As the governor of Kara, he launched a surprise raid on Devagiri (Maharashtra). The Yadavas, caught off guard, failed to mount a strong resistance. Alauddin defeated them and seized a massive treasure. He used the wealth from Devagiri to fund his plan to overthrow his uncle, following a strategy similar to that employed by Mahmud of Ghazni around 200 years earlier.

Fourteen years later, Alauddin's close associate, Malik Kafur Hazardinari, convinced the sultan to launch a new southern military expedition. Kafur subjugated the Kakatiyas of Warangal and the Hoysalas of Dwarasamudra, turning them into vassal states and expanding Alauddin Khalji's empire as far south as the Kaveri River – an achievement unmatched by any ruler since Ashoka. Kafur also raided Madurai, the capital of the Pandyas, but its ruler fled without putting up a fight.

Although the Delhi army plundered the city, they eventually withdrew without forcing the Pandyas to accept vassal status. After their departure, the Pandya ruler returned to Madurai, ensuring that Tamil Nadu remained outside Alauddin Khalji's empire.

In the north, Alauddin's atrocities were more pronounced. He dismembered several kingdoms and forcibly married multiple royal women. However, he should be credited with protecting India from several raids by the barbaric Mongols. Alauddin, nevertheless, died early at the age of 49 due to an illness.

Rise of Vijayanagara

Of his two sons, Mubarak Shah established himself in power. His infatuation with his uterine brother Khusrau Khan, believed to be a former Hindu, proved to be his weakness.

Though Khusrau Khan played a key role in eroding the power of the Kakatiya and Hoysala dynasties, he had the sultan killed in a palace intrigue, thus ending the line of Alauddin Khalji. He then became the sultan, but the Khalji loyalists killed him within two months.

Ghiyath al-Din Tughlaq, the founder of the Tughlaq dynasty, succeeded Khusrau Khan, the exterminator of the Khalji family. However, within six years, he was killed, and his son, Mohammad Bin Tughlaq, became sultan.

Mohammad Bin Tughlaq further expanded his empire by ending the southern dynasties. His inconsiderate policy decisions created unrest among the people. His decision to shift the capital to Devagiri, or Daulatabad, led to the establishment of another Muslim power centre in the south.

His policy of Hindu persecution resulted in the creation of the Vijayanagara kingdom by Harihara Raya and Bukka Raya, which insulated southern India from Muslim powers for nearly 270 years.

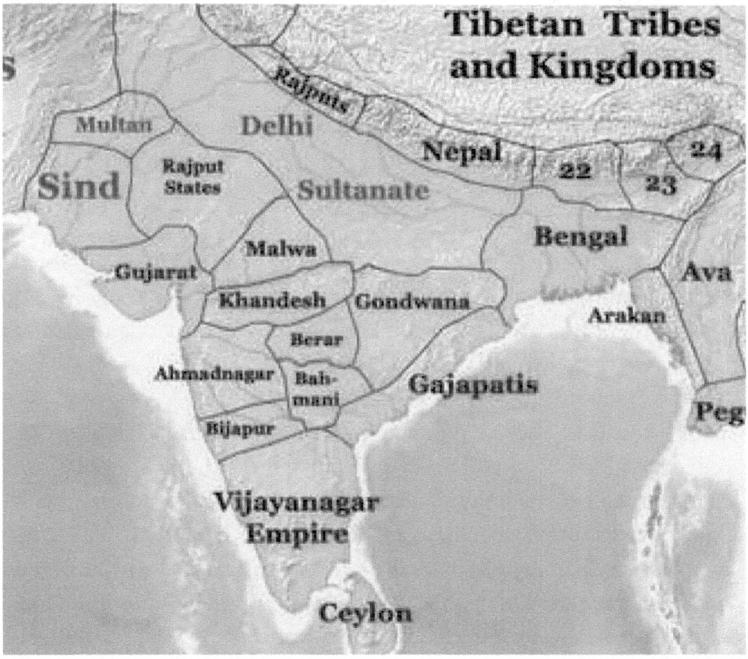

A few years later, Muslim nobles in Devagiri (or Daulatabad) revolted against Mohammad Bin Tughlaq for appointing a low-born man, Aziz Himar, as governor. Later, they defeated the Delhi army and declared the independence of the territory south of the Narmada as the Bahmani Sultanate.

The emergence of the Vijayanagara kingdom, which extended up to the river Krishna, and the Bahmani Sultanate, which controlled the land between the rivers Krishna and Narmada, led to a twin-power scenario prevalent in the south in history.

Timur's raid

At the close of the 14th century, Timur invaded northern India and ransacked Delhi, leaving mountains of bodies piled up in the city. Delhi could not recover from its devastation for the next 100 years.

Many regions, including Gujarat, Punjab, Awadh, and Mewar, rejected Delhi's overlordship. As these regions broke away, the Delhi Sultanate shrank significantly and weakened.

In 1413, after the death of the last Tughlaq ruler, Timur appointed Khizr Khan as the new Delhi Sultan, thus establishing the Sayyid dynasty in Delhi. Over the next 30 years, three rulers changed, and their reigns were largely uneventful.

While the north was in political turmoil, religious syncretism was underway. Several religious personalities emerged from Hinduism, defying ritualistic practices and allowing devotees to connect with God through simpler means, such as chanting. His name or singing His praises. Chaitanya Mahaprabhu in Odisha, as well as Kabir and Vallabhacharya in Uttar Pradesh, propagated their views on God. While they were reforming Hinduism, another guru arose in Punjab

– Guru Nanak – who set out to establish a new religion, the youngest in India: Sikhism. His teachings revolved around the oneness of God and incorporated the best practices of both Hinduism and Islam. The religion was initially pacifist and aimed at self-discovery to connect with God through service.

Weakened north

In the south, the Vijayanagara Empire expanded to cover the entire land between the river Krishna and the southernmost tip of Kanyakumari. The rulers of Vijayanagara and Bahmani frequently fought for control of the Raichur Doab, which lay between the rivers Krishna and Tungabhadra. While both kingdoms flourished economically, Vijayanagara became the largest empire in India and a safe haven for classical Hinduism.

The Lodhi dynasty came to power in Delhi in 1451. Three sultans ruled Delhi over 75 years. By the turn of the new century, however, the Rajputs regained their striking power. They rallied around Rana Sanga of Mewar, and the combined Rajput forces defeated Ibrahim Lodi, the last ruler of his dynasty in Delhi.

Mughal rule begins

When Daulat Khan, the governor of the Punjab region, heard about Ibrahim Lodi's plan to strip him of his post, he invited Babur to invade Delhi, which had once been the possession of his ancestor Timur.

Babur, who had failed to establish his rule in Samarkand, borrowed troops from Persia and the Turks and attacked Delhi. The use of smaller artillery helped Babur defeat Lodi's exceptionally large army.

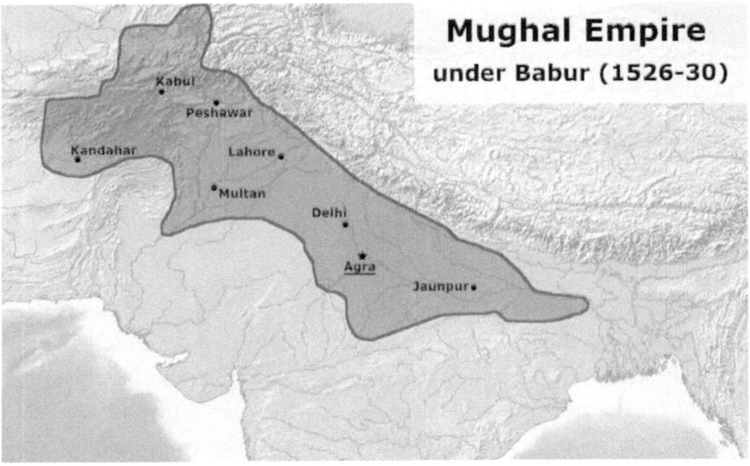

Later, he also defeated a combined Rajput army led by Rana Sanga, firmly establishing Mughal rule in India.

In the south, the Bahmani Sultanate fragmented into five kingdoms: the Nizamshahi of Ahmednagar, the Qutb Shahi of Golconda (Hyderabad), the Barid Shahi of Bidar, the Imad Shahi of Berar, and the Adil Shahi of Bijapur.

The Vijayanagara Empire, on the other hand, grew increasingly prosperous. It became the first Indian kingdom to establish contact with a European power, the Portuguese, and to utilise their military expertise.

Fall of Vijayanagara

In the north, Babur stabilised Mughal rule in India but did not have enough time to make any significant contributions. He died in 1530. His son Humayun faced revolts and became a wanderer. However, when he finally reclaimed his kingdom from Sikandar Suri, he died

soon after in an accidental fall. His minor son, Akbar, was declared his successor. In the south, the Vijayanagara Empire flourished both economically and militarily. The Deccan sultans were no match for their imposing neighbour's might. The prosperity of Vijayanagara reached its peak under Krishnadeva Raya.
Under Rama Raya, the successor and son-in-law of Krishnadeva Raya, the Vijayanagara Empire pushed the Deccan sultans into an existential crisis. Rama Raya skilfully played the Deccan sultans against one another.

Fearing for their survival, the Deccan sultans eventually united their armies against Vijayanagara. Internal sabotage by two Muslim generals of Rama Raya led to the premature end of Vijayanagara's glorious epoch. Rama Raya was beheaded, and his capital, Hampi, was plundered. His brother fled the battlefield with a contingent of troops beyond the Cauvery to regroup.

Although the Vijayanagara rulers continued to govern Mysore, Tamil Nadu, and parts of Kerala from Penukonda, the empire became a pale shadow of its past. Feudatories grew powerful, transforming Vijayanagara into a confederacy rather than an empire.

Mughals take root

In the north, Akbar consolidated his rule by either integrating the Rajputs into his administration or subduing them on the battlefield. Except for a few rulers like Maharana Pratap, most Rajput leaders became part of the Mughal administration. Akbar's strategy ended an 800-year-long struggle between Muslim invaders and Rajput kings, laying a strong foundation for the Mughal Empire.

Having secured the north, Akbar shifted his focus to the south. After an initial defeat, the Mughals managed to occupy Berar and

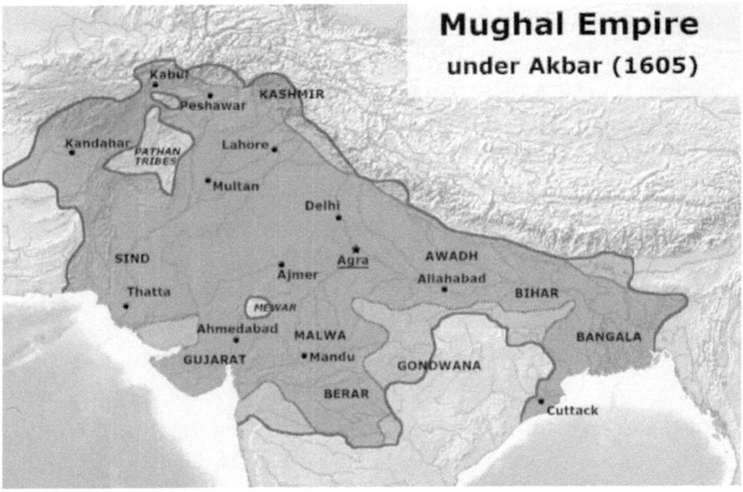

Ahmednagar, the northernmost of the Deccan Sultanates.
The Mughal Empire remained stable and prosperous under Jahangir and his son Shah Jahan. While they faced minor territorial challenges in Kabul, they steadily expanded southward, extracting tribute from Bijapur and Golconda.

Further south, the Nayaka dynasty in Madurai, one of the feudatories of the Vijayanagara kingdom, grew more powerful and became virtually independent of central authority.

Rise of Sikhs

During the reigns of Jahangir and Shah Jahan, Mughal relations with the Sikhs deteriorated. While Akbar had appreciated the work of the Sikh gurus, Jahangir began to see them as a threat. Over the previous century, the Sikhs had evolved into a major organised social group in Punjab, a region that influenced two key Mughal cities: Delhi and Lahore.

The trigger for imperial action against the Sikhs was Guru Arjan's blessing of Prince Khusrau, who had rebelled against Emperor Jahangir. After Khusrau's defeat, Jahangir imprisoned Guru Arjan and gave him an ultimatum: convert to Islam or die. When Guru Arjan refused to convert, he was executed. This event marked a turning point for the Sikhs, as the next guru, Guru Hargobind, began the militarisation of the community, transforming them into a martial class.

Mughal's downfall

The rise of Aurangzeb as Mughal emperor destabilised the balance that Akbar had established in the country. Aurangzeb's policy of territorial expansion brought nearly the entire Indian subcontinent under Mughal rule – only the third time in history after the Mauryas and Alauddin Khalji.

However, Aurangzeb's southern campaigns triggered strong resistance against Mughal rule. This resistance was led by the Marathas, with Shivaji at the forefront. Shivaji, a master of guerrilla warfare, posed a significant challenge to Mughal authority. His greatness lies in the fact that he managed to establish a new kingdom with limited resources, defying the world's largest economy, which India had become under Aurangzeb.

The Maratha resistance forced Aurangzeb to spend most of his time in the Deccan, effectively making Ahmednagar his capital. Had he not expanded his empire to the south, the Mughal Empire might have survived longer. Weakened by constant battles, the Mughal Empire declined further. After his death, the Marathas, under the Peshwa, occupied Maharashtra, Gujarat, and most of central India, adding to the list of empires that the south had weakened and eventually destroyed in the north.

Final nail

By Aurangzeb's time, the Sikhs had emerged as an exceptional martial class, causing concern among both the Mughals and nearby rajas. Efforts were made to curb the growth of Sikhism through various means. The persecution of Sikhs by the Mughals intensified further during the reign of Farrukhsiyar

The final blow to Mughal rule in India came from the Afghan ruler Nadir Shah, who plundered Delhi. After this defeat, several Mughal governors, including those in Hyderabad and Bengal, became virtually independent of Mughal control.

Rise of Marathas

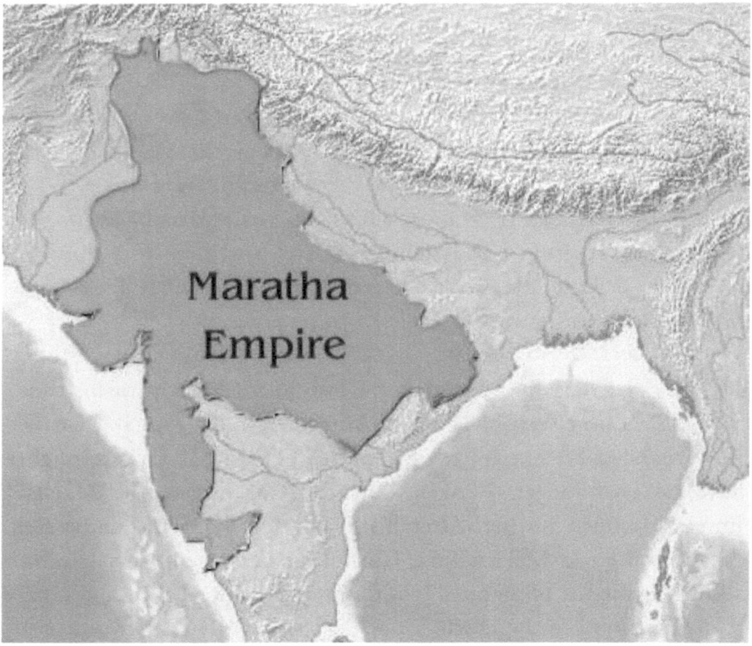

The decline of the Mughal Empire allowed the Marathas to emerge as the preeminent power in the country, nearly 900 years after the Rashtrakutas had played a similar role in national politics. Unlike the centuries-long dominance of the Rashtrakutas in ancient India, the Marathas' glory was short-lived. They were defeated by Afghanistan's Ahmed Shah Abdali, severely diminishing their power projection. As Lahore was under Abdali's rule, the Sikhs bore the brunt of his persecution, which eventually compelled them to establish their own kingdom.

Power brokers

The lack of a central authority forced every ruler to defend their own territory. Some, like Hyder Ali, who had risen through the ranks, were capable of doing so. However, rulers like the successors of the first Nizam, who had little battlefield experience, required external support. French governor Dupleix recognised this need and offered his services, becoming one of the most influential Europeans in India.

Confident in their influence over native powers, the French attacked and occupied the English settlement in Madras as part of the Anglo-French war in Europe. Though they withdrew after the intervention of the Nawab of Arcot, the English realised the importance of political power and backed Muhammad Ali against his rival Chanda Sahib.

Chanda Sahib ended the rule of the Madurai Nayakas in 1736 and established himself as the nawab of central and southern Tamil Nadu, bringing this region under direct Muslim rule for the first time ever.

At the request of local leaders (and on the advice of the British) to restore the old Hindu Madurai Nayaka kingdom, the Marathas arrived in Tamil Nadu to weaken Chanda Sahib. The English allied with the Marathas to defeat Chanda Sahib, who was supported by the

French. The outcome was inevitable – Chanda Sahib could not withstand the might of the Marathas. Mohammad Ali, who was backed by the British, became the Nawab of Arcot, giving the English East India Company its first taste of power.

British rule begins

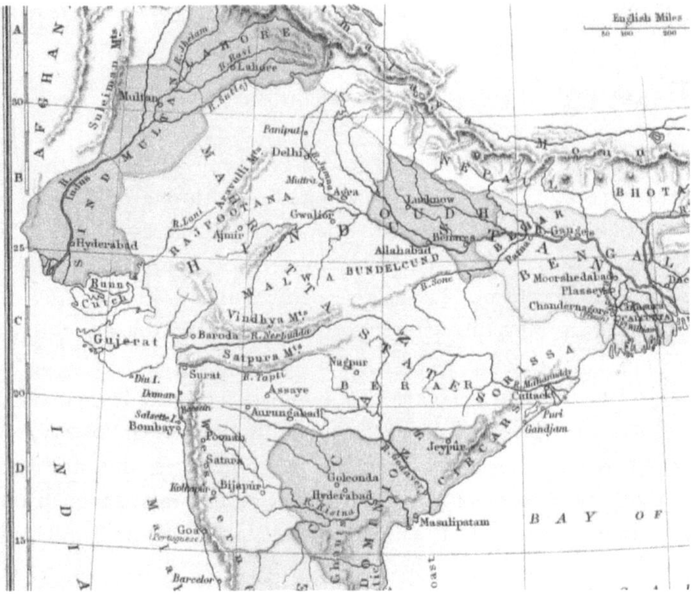

After the French attacks, the British sought to raise fortifications. Having dealt directly with the Mughal Emperor's court, the British failed to accord the required heft to Bengal's Nawab, Sirajuddaula. The Nawab opposed the fortifications, but the British insisted that they faced a French threat and required them. The British joined hands with Mir Jaffar and local bankers to depose the Nawab.

However, Sirajuddaula jailed 100 British officials and captured

Calcutta. Incensed by this, the British ordered reinforcements from Madras under Robert Clive. The Nawab of Arcot, Mohammad Ali, showed his gratitude to the English for elevating him by funding their Bengal expedition. Robert Clive defeated Sirajuddaula and established the English East India Company as one of the major powers in India, alongside the Marathas, Hyder Ali, and the Nizam.

United front

With Bengal and the Carnatic firmly under its control, the graph of British power grew steeply. It outmanoeuvred the French in Hyderabad and reduced the Nizam to a dependent. The British used one native power against another for their benefit.

By 1779, native powers realised the duplicity of the British East India Company. The Nizam of Hyderabad proposed to the Marathas an anti-British confederacy to overthrow the British from India. Hyder Ali also sought similar help against the British through his emissaries. While the northern kings had fought Muslim invaders the most from the 7th to the 15th century, the responsibility of fighting the British fell on rulers south of the Vindhyas, such as the Marathas, the Nizam, and Mysore.

An influential Maratha minister, Nana Phadnavis, in consultation with key generals, drew up a Quadrilateral Anti-British Confederacy involving the Marathas, the Nizam of Hyderabad, Hyder Ali of Mysore, and the Bhonsles of Nagpur. The plan assigned specific actions to each member, which were to be executed simultaneously to paralyse the British and expel them from India. According to the plan, the Marathas would attack Bombay and Surat, the Nizam would block the Vijayawada route to prevent communication between Calcutta and Madras, and Hyder Ali would attack Madras. Ahead of time, the Bhonsles of Nagpur were to go to Puri to collect Chauth and Sardeshmukhi from Odisha. Once attacks were activated elsewhere, the Bhonsles were to target Fort William in Calcutta and lay it to waste.

The confederacy was a great idea. If it had been implemented as designed, India could have been freed from the British in 1779 itself, denying them the engine to become a global superpower. The world would have been different from what it is now. But it did not happen.

The Bhonsles of Nagpur proved to be the weak link in the plan. Due to their long-standing animosity towards the Peshwas, they leaked the plan to the British and began negotiations for a favourable deal. The British bribed Nagpur's ministers to prolong their stay in Odisha. They reached out to the Nizam and offered him a financial bailout and the restoration of Guntur. The Nizam, the original proposer of the plan, silently withdrew. While the Marathas and Hyder Ali did their part, it was not enough to overthrow the British.

Counter operations

The British realised the combined might of Indian rulers and hastened their actions to uproot them. Their first target was Mysore. Though the Marathas and the Nizam had larger armies, they managed them conservatively. Hyder Ali, on the other hand, adopted European military strategies and was a more potent adversary. However, the Marathas had no issues with Hyder Ali, as he had already agreed to the river Krishna as a border. Within the next three years, however, Hyder Ali died of cancer.

His son and successor, Tipu Sultan, was aggressive and lacked diplomacy. His expansionist policies on the Malabar Coast and in Kerala alarmed the Marathas and the Nizam. They joined hands with the

British to defeat him. The Mysore ruler tried to secure French support, but he failed, as they were not ready to open hostilities in Europe. Tipu Sultan also wrote to the Ottomans seeking their help in fighting the British. None of his plans fructified, and three successive wars with the British-led alliance weakened and ultimately killed him. After Tipu's death, the British restored the Wodeyars to the Mysore throne. Even while the British were working to eliminate native powers, a new Sikh kingdom emerged in Punjab in the north. The British, however, did not allow their attention to be diverted from the south.

Marathas' decline

The Marathas were still a major power to contend with in India. The British knew that unless Maratha power was diminished, they could not establish a firm hold in India.

They took advantage of internal conflicts among the Marathas to weaken them. The British intervened on behalf of Raghunath Rao, the younger brother of Balaji Baji Rao, who was overthrown for murdering his minor nephew, Peshwa Narayan Rao.

The seven-year battle (also called the First Anglo-Maratha War, from 1775 to 1782) resulted in a status quo but bound both parties to assisting each other and not aiding their enemies. The Marathas regained most of their territories but promised to support the British against Mysore and to avoid any alliance with the French.

The Second Anglo-Maratha War was triggered by disunity among Maratha generals. After the suicide of Peshwa Sawai Madhav Rao, a 12-member council headed by Nana Phadnavis installed Baji Rao, the son of the fugitive Raghunath Rao, as a puppet Peshwa in 1796. However, after Nana Phadnavis's death four years later, Daulat Rao Scindia took control of the Peshwa's affairs.

The Maratha Confederacy consisted of five key players - the Peshwa of Pune, the Scindias of Gwalior, the Holkars of Indore, the Bhonsles of Nagpur, and the Gaekwads of Baroda. The Peshwa in Pune played the role of conscience keeper and nominal head.

However, after the death of Nana Phadnavis, there was no strong leadership in Pune, allowing Scindia to gain enormous power by controlling both the Peshwa's authority and his army. This was unacceptable to Yashwant Rao Holkar, who marched to Pune with the intention of expelling Scindia's troops. Baji Rao sought Scindia's help, but Holkar defeated their combined army.

Facing defeat on the battlefield, Baji Rao fled Pune and sought asylum from the British. He signed a subsidiary alliance with them, accepting their protection–an act that effectively ended the Maratha Confederacy forever.

Other Maratha generals rejected the deal, as the Peshwa was only a nominal head, which set off the Second Anglo-Maratha War. All the Maratha generals were ultimately defeated and had to cede large parts of their territory to the British.

After 12 years, the Third Anglo-Maratha War was waged. It was fought by the Peshwa's army, supported by the Bhonsles of Nagpur and the Holkars of Indore, against the British. The Scindias of Gwalior and the Gaikwads of Baroda remained neutral. The Marathas were defeated, and the British shifted focused on subduing the Sikhs. With the defeat of both the Marathas and the Sikhs, all institutional hindrances that could have stopped the British from emerging as the paramount power in India were eliminated.

British greed

After the Marathas' defeat, the British East India Company became

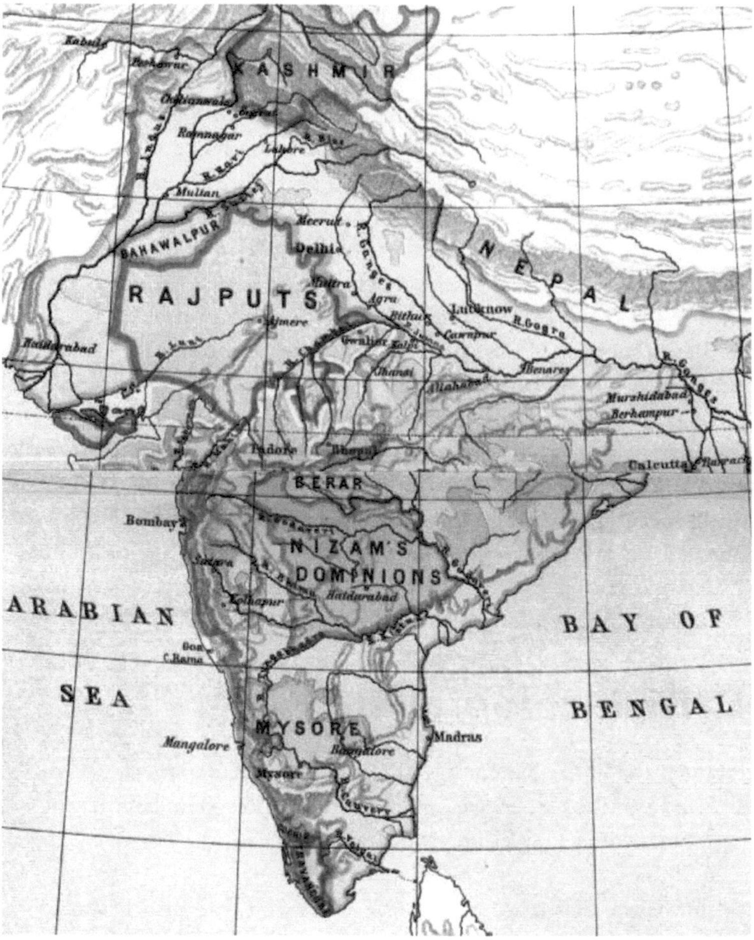

reckless in its pursuit of profit and tried to mould the country to suit its interests, causing widespread distress among the public. Governor-General Dalhousie introduced the Doctrine of Lapse to gradually end the rule of native princes, spreading discontent among the ruling classes. The introduction of cartridges suspected to have covers made with pig and cow fat triggered a revolt in Meerut, which spread like wildfire in Awadh.

The rebel British troops forced a reluctant and aged Mughal Emperor, Bahadur Shah Zafar, to lead them. Subsequently, several rulers of small native states joined the fight against the British, making it one of the few large-scale revolts against colonial rule in India.

Billed as the First War of Independence, the people's organised resistance shocked the British, but the colonial rules soon recovered and ruthlessly suppressed the uprising. It was one of the greatest efforts to rid India of British rule, but it was not supported by the entire south, east, and western regions.

After their victory, the British put an end to even the nominal Mughal presence in India and began to view Muslims with suspicion. The British monarch ended the administration of the East India Company, taking over the reins and suspended further territorial expansion.

British colonialism

In 1861, the Indian Councils Act allowed representatives of non-officials to be part of legislative bodies. Its portfolio system laid the foundations of cabinet government in India.

To prevent a recurrence of the 1857-like revolt, the British administration started installing safety valves for societal pressure. As part of this agenda, it introduced several European administrative measures, including the establishment of lower local courts. The British preferred the use of local languages in these lower courts, which was generally well accepted, except in the United Provinces of Agra and Awadh.

Seeds of partition

Due to the presence of political centres like Agra and Lucknow, this region had a large urban Muslim population. Muslims and the Hindu clerical community, the Kayasthas, had been using Persian, written in the Arabic script, while people in rural areas–mostly Hindus–wrote local languages in the Devanagari script. While urbanites accepted the British decision to drop Persian, they wanted local languages to be written in the Arabic script. However, rural communities, unfamiliar with the Arabic script, preferred Devanagari.

As Hindus lived in villages in great majority, the proposal for Devanagari acquired Hindu colours. Since Muslims were in the majority in urban areas, their demand for the use of the Arabic script was seen as a Muslim demand, though Hindu Kayasthas also supported it. While the issue was essentially about two groups of people fighting to protect their interests in securing employment, it quickly acquired a religious connotation and led to the first communal riots in India under British rule. The thought process of viewing Hindus and Muslims as two distinct nations began with these language-linked communal riots.

Modernising Muslims

Sayyid Ahmad Khan, the son of a noble in the Mughal court, was a pragmatic man. He eschewed dogmatic beliefs in racial superiority and wanted Muslims to accept British rule. As the British believed that Muslims were the real cause of the 1857 revolt, he tried to change this impression of his fellow Muslims.

To escape poverty, he learnt English and joined British service despite coming from a Mughal noble family. When his son became the first Muslim to avail of a government scholarship for Indians to study in

Britain, he visited Oxford and Cambridge and realised the importance of modern education for development.

In 1877, he established the Muhammadan Anglo-Oriental College at Aligarh by pooling donations from several people. The graduates from this college were to become key officials in the 20th century and played a crucial role in the partition of India and the creation of Pakistan.

People's fight begins

Two years later, a major event occurred that would significantly contribute to the rise of a popular national movement. In 1879, Allan Octavian Hume, a senior British civil servant and secretary of the Government of India Secretariat, was summarily removed from his post over some differences regarding "public interest." This incident prompted him to take an active role in fostering the idea of a national movement.

The introduction of the Ilbert Bill in 1883, at the instance of Viceroy Ripon, which empowered Indian judges to try Europeans in the lower courts, invited fierce opposition from Europeans. This reaction galvanised educated Indians against European discrimination. Hume, having already retired from government service, put his ideas into action by writing a letter to the graduates of Calcutta University, urging them to set an agenda for the government.

Indian National Congress

Though several national conferences were conducted by different organisations, the most significant event occurred in late December 1884 in Madras. Seventeen people, including Dadabhai Naoroji from Bombay, Surendranath Banerjee from Calcutta, and S. Subramania

Iyer from Madras, attended the Theosophical Society's annual session at the Mylapore residence of Dewan Bahadur Rai Raghunatha Rao, a prominent Maharashtrian born in Kumbakonam.

During the meeting, they decided to explore the establishment of a national organisation. Hume, who was also a member of the Theosophical Society and was travelling to different cities to meet prominent leaders for the same purpose, could not attend the Madras meeting. However, he met Viceroy Dufferin and convinced him of the need for a safety valve to prevent a repeat of the 1857 revolt. On 27 December 1885, 72 delegates attended the first session of the Indian National Congress in Bombay.

Baby steps

In its initial phase, the Congress focused on securing equal rights for people in India and achieving a greater measure of self-government. Through their efforts, Congress leaders convinced the British to increase the number of non-official members in the Legislative Council in 1892. The Indian Councils Act of 1892 also introduced indirect elections by allowing universities, district boards, municipalities, zamindars, trade bodies, and chambers of commerce to recommend members to the provincial councils. This was considered a victory for the pre-Gandhi Congress.

Fuel to flame

Viceroy Curzon spoiled the relationship between the Congress and the British. He split the unwieldy province of Bengal, a step he took based on several previous recommendations. However, when protests erupted across Bengal, he sought to justify it as a move to create a Muslim-majority state, sowing the seeds of religion-based division in eastern India.

Bengal was ablaze with protests across the state. Vande Mataram became the war cry of the protestors. As a result, demands grew for a more aggressive and combative Congress. However, leaders like Gopal Krishna Gokhale and Pherozeshah Mehta, among others – who were nicknamed the moderates – were not in favour of a combative approach. Bal Gangadhar Tilak, Bipin Chandra Pal, Lala Lajpat Rai, and Aurobindo Ghosh, among others – called extremists – preferred direct action on the streets. As differences grew, the moderates, who were in the majority, expelled the extremists from the Congress at its Surat session in 1907.

Another aftereffect of the strident opposition to the partition of Bengal by educated Bengalis, who were mostly Hindus, was the establishment of the All-India Muslim League in 1906 in Dhaka. However, it remained mostly an elite organisation representing the landed class. The Indian Councils Act of 1909, also known as the Morley-Minto Reforms, introduced the election of representatives through an electoral college of local bodies. Muslims were recognised as a separate electorate. For the first time, an Indian joined the Executive Council of the Governor-General. The powers of the legislative councils were increased. This was hailed as a victory for the moderates.

These concessions, however, failed to satisfy Tilak and other expelled Congress leaders. So, Tilak joined Annie Besant's Home Rule League movement, which demanded dominion status for India within a set timeframe. Mohammad Ali Jinnah was also a member of the Home Rule League. As protests continued in Bengal, the British decided to annul the partition in 1911 to quell dissent. However, as a punishment for the educated Bengalis who had protested, the capital was shifted from Calcutta to New Delhi.

While the popularity of the extremists increased among the people, the top leaders of the moderates either grew old or passed away by

1916. Both factions merged again at the Lucknow session under the presidency of Bal Gangadhar Tilak, when he officially called for Swaraj (freedom).

Agitational policy

While freedom was officially on the Congress agenda, an Indian returning from South Africa was about to change the party forever. Mohandas Karamchand Gandhi, a barrister from London and the son of the dewan of Rajkot, attended the Congress session at Lucknow for the first time as a delegate. He was already popular in India because of his agitations in South Africa.

Gandhi's methods of agitation were entirely different, even compared to the extremists. However, people realised that his methods were effective, as demonstrated in Champaran. Congress sessions had previously been dismissed as a three-day annual festival of educated Indians. Gandhi forced the Congress to increase its contact with the people and successfully transformed the party into a truly national organisation.

The First World War created shortages of every kind across the world. It further increased discontent among people, advancing the Congress's goals. While the British treated India merely as a market, the war forced them to revise their approach and encourage Indian manufacturing units to boost war supplies. This, in turn, led to the emergence of a comparatively larger middle class and a stronger entrepreneurial base.

Hindu-Muslim unity

After their victory in the First World War, the British dismantled the defeated Ottoman Empire, creating several smaller nations, including Turkey, Saudi Arabia, Iraq, Syria, and Lebanon. Adding insult to injury, Turkey's leader, Mustafa Kemal, who was himself a Muslim, abolished the institution of the Caliphate, a position held by the Ottoman emperor as the leader of the Muslim world. Muslims in India blamed the British for the abolition of the Caliphate and organised protests against them.

In an attempt to unify Hindus and Muslims against British rule and counter the colonists' divide-and-rule policy, Gandhi persuaded the Congress to support the Muslims' demand for the restoration of the Caliphate. Though Mohammad Ali Jinnah opposed the use of religion in politics, the Congress endorsed the movement. The initiative proved successful, but Jinnah quit the Congress and moved to London to resume his law practice.

Empowered locally

The Government of India Act, 1919, based on the Montagu-Chelmsford reforms, was a response to the growing demand for greater Indian representation in law-making. It introduced direct elections, though voting rights were highly restricted to those who met property, tax, or educational qualifications. The Legislative Council at the Centre was replaced by a bicameral system consisting of an Upper House and a Lower House. Separate electorates, previously granted to Muslims, were now extended to Sikhs, Christians, and Anglo-Indians.

The Act also introduced dyarchy in the provinces, allowing Indians to participate in administration as ministers for people-centric subjects such as public health, education, agriculture, and local self-government. However, finance, law and order, the army, and the police remained under the governor's direct control.

Power to people

India's freedom struggle was long and multifaceted. The Congress launched several agitations, some of which were successful while others were not. Although the Congress remained the primary organisation in the freedom movement, many individuals and groups pursued their own strategies based on their understanding of the situation. Revolutionaries, armed groups, cultural organisations, teachers, and businesspeople contributed by either raising awareness of British atrocities or inspiring people to resist colonial injustice.

As a culmination of these efforts, the British introduced the Government of India Act, 1935, which allowed Indians to join the government through dyarchy at the federal level. The Federal Legislature was to consist of two chambers–the Council of States and the Federal Assembly. Provincial governments were granted autonomy, and communal electorates were extended to include depressed classes, women, and labourers.

Decline of British

The Second World War proved to be a testing time for the British. As Britain's largest overseas territory, India was expected to play a major role in the war effort. While Indian industries provided full support, the Congress made its cooperation conditional on immediate independence for India. The British rejected this demand and proceeded with their war efforts without further consultation.

As a result, when the Congress launched the "Quit India" movement in August 1942, the British responded by arresting tens of thousands of its leaders. However, the movement was carried forward by second-rung leaders, reflecting the widespread popularity of the freedom struggle. The Muslim League, however, supported the British's war efforts and became one of the important players in Indian politics.

Subhash Chandra Bose, one of the top Congress leaders, escaped from house arrest and travelled to anti-British countries such as Germany and Japan. He sought their assistance in fighting the British militarily in India. Japan agreed to help him. Bose revived the Indian National Army (INA), which had been set up by Rash Behari Bose in 1942 using Indian prisoners of war in Singapore.

As the British-led Allied forces won the Second World War, 12,000 INA soldiers were captured and brought to Delhi for trial. However, the public viewed them as true patriots, leading to widespread protests across India. Communal divisions temporarily disappeared, and both the Congress and the Muslim League called for the soldiers' release. The Congress, with its greater legal resources, deployed a team of lawyers led by Jawaharlal Nehru to argue against their court-martial.

The revolt of naval ratings in Mumbai became the final blow to British rule in India. Naval ratings went on strike on 18 February 1946, demanding better living conditions. The strike quickly spread to other cities such as Madras, Karachi, and Calcutta, involving 10,000 sailors and 56 ships. Some soldiers of the British Indian Army in Poona and Madras also defied their superiors' orders.

The British, despite having just won the Second World War, deployed a larger force to suppress the rebellion. In an effort to prevent further escalation at a time when independence was imminent, Congress leader Sardar Patel and the Muslim League's Jinnah intervened. The naval ratings surrendered, and some were dismissed on 25 February. However, this incident shattered British confidence in the loyalty of Indian troops.

Transfer of power

Within a month, on 14 March 1946, the British government offered independence to India. The formal process for Indian independence began on 16 May 1946, when the British government issued a report recommending the formation of an interim government to draft a constitution.

In 1946, a Cabinet Mission arrived in India to discuss the transfer of power from the British government to Indian political leaders. The mission aimed to preserve India's unity while granting it independence. It proposed a unified India with a weak federal government, giving significant autonomy to individual states. Both the Congress and the Muslim League accepted the plan.

However, a month later, Jawaharlal Nehru rejected the idea of states forming into groups, which was the key demand of the Muslim League, and asserted that the Constituent Assembly will not be bound by the Cabinet Mission plan. This led to the Muslim League's Direct Action Day, which led to the death of thousands of people.

The Congress formed an interim government in September 1946 to eventually take over the reins of India from the British. Though the Muslim League initially refused to join the interim government, it joined it and created hindrances to its functioning. The deadlock was ultimately resolved through the partition of India, leading to the creation of a new Muslim-majority nation, Pakistan.

The partition resulted in unprecedented communal violence in Punjab and Bengal. Thousands of people were massacred, leaving deep and lasting scars on the Indian psyche. On 14th August 1947, Pakistan became independent.

A day later, on 15th August, India achieved its hard-earned liberation, making its people, in Rabindranath Tagore's words, India's *Bhagya Vidhatas* (makers of destiny).

Bibliography

1. *Global Tectonics,* Philip Kearey, Keith A. Klepeis, Frederick J. Vine

2. Liviu Giosan, Climate of the Past, Nov. 13, 2018

3. *Socio Economic Life Of India In The Vedic Period,* Haripada Chakraborty

4. *The Vedic Age and the Coming of Iron c. 1500-700 BC,* Irfan Habib & Vijay Kumar Thakur

5. *The Invasion of India by Alexander, the Great,* J.W. M'crindle

6. *The Age of The Nandas and Mauryas,* Prof. H. C.. Raychaudhuri

7. *History of Tamils from earliest times to 600 AD,* P.T. Srinivasa Iyengar

8. *History of the Sunga Dynasty,* Binod Chandra Sinha

9. *The Indo-Greeks,* A.K. Narian

10. *Later Indo-Scythians,* Major Gen. Sir Alex Cunningham

11. *The History of Satavahanas and Western Kshatrapas,* VV Mirashi

12. *India under The Kushanas,* B.N. Puri

13. *The Gupta Empire,* Radhakumud Mookerji

14. *Vakataka Gupta Age,* R.C. Majumdar, Anant Sadashiv Altekar

15. *Abhiras: Their History and Culture,* Bhagwansingh Survavanshi

16. *Kadamba Kula,* George M. Moraes

17. *Kalabhra Interregnum: Retrospect and Prospect,* B.G.L. Swamy

18. *History of Malwa,* Sukhsampattirai Bhandari

19. *Harshacharita*, P.V. Kane
20. *Hunnic Peoples in Central and South Asia Sources for their Origin and History*, Daniel Balogh

21. *Political History of the Chalukyas of Badami*, Durga Prasad Dikshit

22. *Studies In Pallava History*, Rev. H. Heras, S. J.

23. *Kashir: A History of Kashmir*, G. M. D. Sufi

24. *The History Of The Gurjara Pratiharas*, Baij Nath Puri

25. *Rashtrakutas and Their Times*, Altekar, A.S.

26. *A History of Afghanistan*, Brig. Gen. Sir Percy Sykes

27. *The Chalukyas Of Kalyana And The Kalachuris*, B.R Gopal

28. *Cholas I*, K. A. Nilakanta Sastri

29. *Proceedings of the Indian History Congress, Vol. 3 (1939)*, N. Venkataramanayya

30. *The Life and Times of Sultan Mahmud of Ghazna*, Muhammad Nazim

31. *The Struggle For Empire*, R.C. Majumdar

32. *'Silhouette of South Indian History, Archaeology, Epigraphy, Culture and Tourism'*, K. V. Ramakrishna Rao

33. *The Paramaras (800-1305)*, Pratipal Bhatia

34. *Chaulukyas of Gujarat*, Asoke Kumar Majumdar

35. *History of the Chahamanas*, R.B. Singh

36. *Palas of Bengal*, R.D. Banerji

37. *The Sultanate of Delhi (711-1526)*, A.L. Srivastava

38. *The Foundation of Muslim Rule in India,* A.B.M. Habibullah
39. *The Seunas (The Yadavas of Devagiri),* Shrinivas Ritti

40. *The Kakatiyas of Warangal,* Dr P.V. Parabrahma Sastry

41. *The Hoysala Vamsa,* William Coelhi

42. *A Forgotten Empire Vijayanagar,* Sewell Robert

43. *Bahmani Kingdom,* Major J.S. King

44. *Timur, the Great Amir,* J.H. Sanders

45. *The Mughal Empire,* A.L. Srivastava

46. *The History of the Sikhs, Vol. 1,* Hari Ram Gupta

47. *Shivaji and His Times,* Sir Jadunath Sarkar

48. *The Fall of the Mughal Empire,* Sir Jadunath Sarkar

49. *British Relations With Haidar Ali 1760-1782,* B. Sheikh Ali

50. *The Rise and Fall of the Maratha Empire,* N.R. Vyankatesh

51. *Dupleix,* Col. G.B. Malleson

52. *Dupleix and Clive: The Beginning of Empire,* Henry Dodwell

53. *Considerations on the Conquest of Tanjore and The Restoration of the Rajah,* Records of the East India Company

54. *The Life of Lord Robert Clive,* Sir John Malcolm

55. *History Of The Marathas Vol-3,* Govind Sakharam Sardesai

56. *Haidar Ali and Tipu Sultan,* Lewin B. Bowring

57. *Retrospects and Prospects of Indian Policy,* Major Evans Bell

58. *The First War of Indian Independence,* Vinayak Damodar

Savarkar
59. *A History of Sepoy War in India Vol. 1, 2, 3,* John William Kaye

60. *The History of British India under Company and Crown,* P.E. Roberts

61. *One Language, Two Scripts: The Hindi Movement in Nineteenth Century North India*, Christopher R. King

62. *The Life And Work Of Sir Syed Ahmed Khan,* George F. Irving

63. *Allan Octavian Hume: Father of the Indian National Congress, 1829-1912,* William Wedderburn

64. *India Under Rippon,* Wilfrid Scawen Blunt

65. *How India Wrought For Freedom,* Annie Besant

66. *The Development of Self-Government in India, 1858-1914,* Cecil Merne Putnam Cross

67. *India under Curzon & After,* Lovat Fraser

68. *Congress and Congressmen In The Pre- Gandhian Era (1885-1917),* Bhakat Prasad Mazumdar

69. *Indian National Congress (1885-1935),* B. Pattabhi Sitaramayya

70. *The Khilafat Movement in India 1919-1924,* A. Niemeijer

71. *Political India 1935-1942,* Anatomy of Indian Politics

72. *Muslim Politics (1906-1942),* Humayun Kabir

73. *The Cabinet Mission in India,* A.C. Banerjeee

74. *The Transfer of Power In India,* V.P.Menon

OTHER PUBLICATIONS

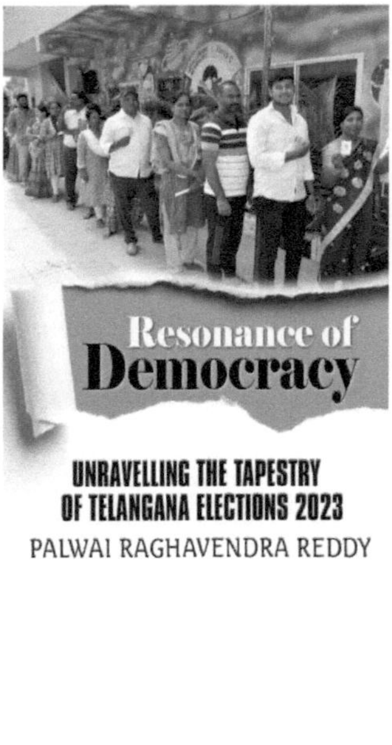

ABOUT AUTHOR

S. Mahesh (S. Umamaheshwar) is a senior journalist from Hyderabad and a history scholar from Osmania University. He has been working with Deccan Chronicle newspaper since 2002 and wrote on several topics such as business, investment, banking, personal finance, and economic policy. He also won Shriram Sanlam Award for Excellence in Financial Journalism in 2016. He authored a historical fiction 'Roving Eyes - Love, Lust and Battles of Indian Royalty'.

www.ingramcontent.com/pod-product-compliance
Ingram Content Group UK Ltd.
Pitfield, Milton Keynes, MK11 3LW, UK
UKHW041352190726
13845UKWH00026B/565

9 788197 053405